LESSONS LEARNED ON THE SEAT OF MY BUS

LESSONS LEARNED ON THE SEAT OF MY BUS

Secrets to enjoying life no matter what happens!

PAUL WAGLER

© Copyright 2015 – Paul Wagler
3rd Edition
All rights reserved.

This book may not be copied or reprinted for commercial gain or profit. Scripture quotations are from the New International Version of the Bible, unless otherwise indicated.

Cover Design by Angie Wagler
Thanks to Editing Team:
Don Boyd, John Turner and Angie Wagler

ISBN-13: 978-1517570163
ISBN-10: 1517570166

ENDORSEMENTS

Paul writes from such a unique perspective bringing insight and humor into everyday life. Buckle your seat belt and enjoy the ride in reading this treasure.

– Brian Fleming, Author, "Your Life Matters"

I can't stop laughing from the stories in your book! I'm sitting here alone in the living room just laughing out loud! Good job!

– Judith Ann Martin

Really great book! When is the next one?

– Daniel Jutzi

Oh, Paul – you have hit the nail on the head. This book is so much fun! I love "Where you are seated determines your perspective." Each of the sections starts off like a tasty appetizer – and ends up with a nourishing nugget of God's truth. I look forward to your "Seat of the Bicycle" book.

> **– Jane Huff, Author "An Intimate Look at the Armor of God"**

Paul, I just finished reading your book and by the end I had tears. I found myself in so many of these situations; I felt you wrote the book just for me. Thank you Paul for this inspiring and enjoyable read and I will "Let it Go."

> **– Audrey Mayhew**

This book is captivating, encouraging and truly inspiring. "I seek to make right choices in every situation because of this great love" is a statement that resonated with me in a powerful way! Paul is an authentic writer with a keen ability to connect with the heart of the reader through depth of wisdom and revelation encountered through his everyday life and professional journey. His understanding on perspective, destination and purpose have been of great value to me, as I know will be for many others, as he presents these with practical applications that bring transformation!

> **– Claudia Santiago, International Recording Artist, Speaker, Author, Consultant and CEO of Viva-La-Vida! Success**

Just finished. This was exceptionally enlightening. Thanks.

> **– Tariq Deonandan**

WOW! Paul you've done real good. Your book is packed with good points to lead an abundant life.

— *Thys De Jong*

Just read an amazing book called "Lessons Learned on the Seat of My Bus." What an awesome book to read!

— *David Sej*

THANKS TO:

Angie

– my wonderful life partner. You have always been such an encouragement to me. Your love for God and passion to follow the call on our lives is inspiring! As one prophet recently told me, "I am who I am because of you."

My parents

– for showing me what it is like to pursue God with all your heart. You both have been a great support for all of my years.

Wayne & Mary Wagler
– for mentoring Angie and me when we first started in ministry. Your ongoing encouragement has been invaluable.

Marc Leacock and the Christian Link
– for providing a setting for God to bring me back to life and start to dream again.

Tamara Lowe, Steve Kasyanenko and the whole Christian Experts community
– for all the encouragement to "go for it" and just get started.

Don & Sharon Boyd
– for your timely words of encouragement that have kept me on the journey. And Don – for your editing gift and willingness to help with that process.

Roger Bowman
– For the invitation to speak at the men's breakfast meeting that got me started on my "Lessons Learned" series of talks.

Grand River Transit and all my wonderful co-workers
– who help to make this a wonderful job!

TABLE OF CONTENTS

Preface...15

Introduction...19

Chapter 1 - The Seat..31

Chapter 2 - The Sign..49

Chapter 3 - The System......................................73

Chapter 4 - The Secret..83

Conclusion..99

About Paul & Angie Wagler..............................101

One Last Thing..103

PREFACE

I want to start to by giving thanks for the goodness of God! Over and over, as I go through life, I am in awe and overwhelmed with how good God is. This is the central theme of scripture from the beginning to the end of the Bible. I love Psalm 34:8 where we are told to, "taste and see that the Lord is good." This is not just a theory or something that we hope is true. Instead, we are invited to experience it first hand. I want to declare I have tasted and I know that God is good! It has become the theme of my life, and I realize without the goodness of God I don't know where I would be.

As I live my life, I am often thinking of what I can learn from what's happening around me; and, more specifically, as a preacher, how I can use this experience in a sermon. It's just the way I'm wired – always thinking of practical examples to help communicate life lessons and make the teachings in the Bible relevant to our life today.

As I read the Bible and the things Jesus taught, I realize that He did the same thing. Jesus regularly taught using parables – earthly stories with a heavenly meaning. He would start by saying, "The Kingdom of God is like…" Then he would proceed to tell a story about a farmer who went out to sow seeds, a king who had servants, a man who had two sons, and many other everyday stories to which people could relate.

This book that you are about to read is a modern day parable. As I have worked at my job as transit bus driver for the last 14 years, I have learned things that can be applied to many areas of life. These life-lessons have helped me to understand the teachings of the Bible as well. I think that, if there were such as thing as a transit bus 2,000 years ago, Jesus might have said, "The Kingdom of God is like a man who went out to drive his bus."

My hope is that this book will bring great encouragement to everyone who reads it! If you feel stuck in your life and you need a change in perspective, then this book is for you. I believe that using examples from the seat of the bus will also bring understanding to the teachings of Bible in an easy to understand kind of way.

One of the goals of my life is to enjoy every day to fullest! This is one of my passions, and I desire to help others live in this fullness as well. "Yesterday is gone, and tomorrow may never come," are the words of a song, and the reality in which we all live. Today is all we have. If we don't enjoy today, we have lost something we can never get back. What I will share in the following pages of this book are the ways in which I have learned to enjoy life every day.

INTRODUCTION

I love my job as a bus driver! I love driving; and I love relating to people, so it's the perfect combination.

Before I started driving bus, I served as a pastor in a local church. As I was driving bus around the city, I began to think about how the job of driving bus and being a pastor are similar and how they are different. Here is one example of each.

Similarity

When you are a bus driver, time is very important. People need to know what time the bus is coming so they can plan their trip. The bus needs to stay on schedule, as much as possible, to provide a reliable service to the customers. As a driver, I am always aware of what time it is; as are the many customers who are checking the time frequently to make sure they will make their connection or destination on time.

Somewhat surprising, are the customers who don't have a clue about what time it is; they are just kind of "winging" their way through life. Actually, some don't even seem to know the day of the week or what month it is, either. One time, I told a lady that her previous month's bus pass was no longer valid on the 7th day of the current month. Her response was, "You guys never told me it was a new month!"

Introduction

For a pastor time is also important. When preaching a sermon, people in the congregation may be checking their watches to see if the pastor is on schedule. This meeting is supposed to be done by 12:00, and I have to be somewhere by 12:30. "This guy is only half done his sermon; we are going to be late, and I will miss my 'connection,'" is what is going through some minds while listening to the sermon. So, as a pastor and a bus driver, time and helping people make their connections are very similar.

Difference

When people come on the bus, quite often, they tend to gather around the front. I regularly need to ask people to move in, as there is lots of room toward the back. I'm not sure exactly why this happens. Could it be that the bus driver smells so good? There is a door at the back of the bus, but there just seems to be something about the front door.

In church, people tend to avoid the front rows like it isn't safe to sit there. In most church meetings I have attended, the front row or two is empty while the back rows are full. The thinking must be that being closer to the exit is better so a quick escape can easily be made. Some years ago, in the church that I was leading, I decided to mix things up one Sunday morning. We met in a community center where we had to set up chairs every week. So, at the start of the sermon, I went to the back of the room and asked everyone to turn their chairs around. The back row became the front row! Seems like the Kingdom of God when Jesus said, "The last shall be first, and the first shall be last."

The Daily life of a Bus Driver

The task of driving a transit bus around the city has proved to be a very interesting experience. A bus driver deals with all kinds of situations throughout the course of the day. Not only do

Introduction

we deal with all different kinds of customers; but we also have to contend with traffic, pedestrians, cyclists, trying to stay on schedule, construction, and all kinds of weather. Then, with all these factors to deal with, we need to provide excellent customer service and answer questions all day long!

When a transit bus drives down the street, it has a ripple affect on its surroundings; like when a boat is moving in the water, it creates a wake. If you are in a canoe and a boat is coming, you need to position yourself so that the wake does not overturn your canoe. Similarly, when you are around a bus, you need to position yourself properly because strange things happen around buses. I often feel that like a boat; I'm leaving a wake as a drive down the street. Occasionally, this is actually literally happening when there are large puddles, or in some cases, small ponds on the road due to heavy rain. There have been times, due to storm drains being backed up, that

I have driven my bus through water so deep it was coming in the doors of my bus.

Quite often, when my bus turns onto a street and people see me, they start to run. No, they aren't running to get away because they are scared of the bus. Instead, they are running because they want to catch the bus; and they are not at the bus stop. These people will do crazy and unexpected things, just to make sure they catch the bus. Oh, the stories every bus driver could tell about the close calls they have seen! People will risk their lives by darting through traffic, or even worse, by running out, right in front of the bus. So, where there is a bus, watch out because people do some really surprising things.

Another effect a bus has on it's surroundings is with the wonderful "4 wheelers," or cars, as they are commonly known. When there is a bus on the road, every car that is behind it wants to be in front of it. In many cases, these

Introduction

cars will try anything to get in front of the bus. This creates many challenging situations. Again, every bus driver could tell you dozens of stories of close calls or actual accidents with cars. The most common situation is a car passes the bus only to turn right immediately, causing the need for sudden braking, an increased heart rate, and some muttering under your breath. At least we hope it stays under our breath!

If you are not a bus driver and you're reading this book, you probably have some of your own bus stories to tell. These may be stories where a bus has cut you off or done something else to annoy you. These things occasionally do happen; and I apologize on behalf of all bus drivers, as we are not perfect.

Interesting customers

As a bus driver, you meet all sorts of people! The many interesting customers I have met over the years have helped to make this job quite enjoyable. I have always liked the senior citizens that consider it their purpose in life to help bus drivers keep their sugar level high. Several of these precious people regularly give us some kind of candy or chocolate. Some days, they appear at just the right time – kind of like angels. I'm feeling a bit drowsy and I see the wonderful Portuguese lady waiting; and I say, "YES!" There was one older gentleman who we called, "the Werther's Man," as he would regularly give us a handful of Werther candies.

One time, as I neared the stop where this lady was going to get off, she asked me if I was married. I said, "Yes, and happily married." She then told me to tell my wife that a 75-year-old lady just fell in love with me. I was a bit taken a back and thought, "Okay; I will make sure I tell my wife, as I'm sure she will be quite concerned!"

There used to be a certain mother and son

Introduction

that would ride the bus together. The little boy would love to stand close to the driver and watch everything that we did while operating the bus. One day when the son was about 7 years old, he noticed how hairy my arms are. Let me just say that, one of the unique things about me is how much hair I have on my arms and hands. Something doesn't seem right in the universe when a man can't grow hair on the top of his head, where everyone wants it to grow; but he can grow hair everywhere else. Anyway, back to the story. So he noticed my arms and said, "Wow! Do you ever have a lot of fur on your arms! You should shave it off like my mother does!" I was shocked; but not as stunned as the mother who stood there speechless!

One time, when I stopped to let someone off the bus, a car pulled in front of me and stopped. My first thought was, "Oh no! What is he upset at me for?" The driver came to my window and told me that I had a guy on roller blades "bumper hitching" on the back of my bus. I guess there is more than one way to get a free ride on a bus. I quickly got out of my seat to check and saw someone roll away from the back of my bus to the other side of the street. I was glad that this story didn't end badly with this guy wiping out behind my bus at 40-50 km/h.

Here's a quick summary of some other interesting experiences I have had while driving a bus. I have twice had people on the roof of my bus; and several times, people have gotten sick on my bus. I've had many screaming children, and, sometimes, screaming parents at the same time, domestic disputes, loud music, drunk people, and some serious mental health issues. Customers and car drivers have threatened me, and I have had people spit at my bus. I have been hit on the side of the bus, on the back of the bus, and in the front of the bus by cars. I also have had numerous buses breakdown on me in lots of different places around the city.

Introduction

In a lot of ways, every day is an adventure when driving a bus!

Chapter 1
THE SEAT

I grew up on farm and lived in the country for the first 32 years of my life. I had never been on a city bus before I started my job as a bus driver. I did, however, have some experiences with these buses over the years, where I was the one who found them to be annoying and wished they would get out of the way. There are some interactions that I had with buses that I remember well.

Lessons Learned on the Seat of My Bus

The first was quite a number of years ago. I was in Ottawa with a youth group from our church on a trip. We rented bicycles to ride around the city. In Ottawa, they have lanes on their roads that have diamonds on them as they are designated for buses and taxis only. Being the country boy that I was, I wasn't aware of what these special lanes were for, and had not driven in a city with these special lanes. While we were biking around the city, I suggested we ride in these diamond lanes, as there was no traffic in them. It seemed to make sense to me. As we are riding along, a bus came up behind us and started honking his horn at us. I thought the bus driver should just relax and wondered what his problem was!

The second experience was also a number of years ago when I was working for a local trucking company. I delivered food to stores and restaurants. One day, I had a delivery to a Hasty Market in downtown London. As I pulled up to the store, I determined that the best spot to park

Chapter 1 — **The Seat**

the truck for the delivery was in the bus stop. When I came out of the store, a bus was waiting; and the driver was honking his horn at me to get out of his bus stop. Again, I thought the driver should just calm down and stop his ruckus.

Along with these experiences as a truck driver, I used to have a strong dislike for city buses. I hated driving behind these buses as all they ever did was stop! If I saw a bus ahead of me I would try to get ahead of it. This wasn't always easy with a truck; and, many times, I had to suffer behind the bus, stopping and starting over and over again!

Now, let's fast forward a few years from these experiences to 2001, when I was hired by Grand River Transit as a bus driver. Now, I was the one sitting in the driver's seat of the annoying city bus!

There was a lot to learn when I began this job. I had to learn all of the routes around the city, how to read driver's itineraries, all the policies and expectations of how we relate to customers, how to navigate around all the different kinds of buses in the fleet, each with their own unique things about them, and how to drive these buses on busy city streets, just to name a few. The learning curve at the start felt like it was pretty steep. I quickly realized, though, that I really liked this job. I would come home and say to Angie, "I think I was made for this job." I love to drive and I love to relate people, as stated earlier; so this job seemed like a perfect fit.

As I drove around the city picking up and dropping off customers and interacting with traffic for over 8 hours every day, I began to see things very differently than I did before. My mind went back to these experiences from years earlier where I was annoyed with city buses; and, suddenly, I had a different perspective on all of this. Now, I was the guy who was honking his horn at people who were parked in my bus stops!

Chapter 1 — **The Seat**

I was honking my horn at cars that were in 'bus only' lanes! I was the guy honking my horn at pedestrians who were jaywalking or walking across the intersection on my advanced green! If I didn't honk my horn at them, I would start to feel agitated about how they were getting in my way. I was also the guy who was now stopping every block at bus stops and holding up traffic. I was just doing the job I was hired to do, and many people that I interacted with daily were annoyed that I was on the same street as they were, or in their neighbourhood!

Then, I had a life-changing revelation:

The world looks different from the seat of the bus!

I now understood why these bus drivers in Ottawa and London had honked at me. They had a job to do, and I had been oblivious to the way I was hindering them. Now, each day,

I experienced many people who seemed to be unaware of how the decisions they made were impacting my ability to do my job. All of the sudden, my perspective had changed. It really is hard to explain, unless you have sat in the driver's seat of a bus for a whole day; but the world really does look different from the seat of a bus.

When this revelation came, I began to ponder if there was more that I could learn from it that relates to the rest of life. I, then, got another level of understanding; and it was this:

Where you are seated determines your perspective!

Where you are seated everyday determines how you view life and all that is happening around you. I view life in the city and what happens on the road very differently than the guy seated in his car behind me, the gal seated on her bicycle seat ahead of me, and the pedestrian walking

Chapter 1 — **The Seat**

down the sidewalk.

What does 'perspective' mean? The dictionary definition is "a way of regarding situations or topics." In a general way, each of us have perspectives on life that come from the life experiences that we have had. In specific situations, what we see is dictated from the place we are in when it happens or, we could say, "where we are seated."

Since we are talking about what happens on the roads, let's look at an accident to help understand this. If there is an accident involving two cars in the middle of an intersection, there is the possibility of a lot of different perspectives on what happened and why it happened. Each of the people involved in the accident will see things uniquely, as will any passengers in the cars involved. There could be several car drivers who saw this from each side of the intersection. As well, there could have been pedestrians on the sidewalk, each of whom will have their own, unique perspective. There may have been someone who saw it all happen from the 10th floor of the office building at that corner. So, in an event like this, there could be a lot of different perspectives as to what actually happened and who is at fault.

One time, a number of years ago, I had a close call with a pedestrian on a rainy day. I started to turn right on a red light and, while I was still turning, the light turned green. A person who was waiting to cross the street started to walk when the light turned green and didn't see my bus because her umbrella was impeding her vision. She nearly walked into the side of my bus. Someone sitting in the traffic line a half a block away saw this and, from their perspective, thought that I almost ran over the pedestrian. This person was so sure their perspective was correct; they drove immediately to the transit headquarters and reported me to the supervisor.

Chapter 1 — The Seat

It was determined, after an investigation, that, indeed, I had not nearly driven over the person, as had been reported.

Remember that where you are seated determines your perspective.

I began to think about this revelation as a follower of Jesus. The Bible has some things to say about where we are seated as Christians. Let's look at two passages of Scripture that relate to this.

Ephesians 2:4-7

> [4] But because of His great love for us, God, who is rich in mercy, [5] made us alive with Christ even when we were dead in transgressions—it is by grace you have been saved. [6] And God raised us up with Christ and seated us with Him in the heavenly realms in Christ Jesus, [7] in order that, in the coming ages, He might show the incomparable riches of His grace, expressed in His kindness to us in Christ Jesus.

Lessons Learned on the Seat of My Bus

Colossians 1:1-3

Since, then, you have been raised with Christ, set your hearts on things above, where Christ is, seated at the right hand of God. ² Set your minds on things above, not on earthly things. ³ For you died, and your life is now hidden with Christ in God.

I love these verses! God has such incredible love for all of us that, before we made the move toward Him, He sent Jesus to this Earth so you and I could all be "made alive in Christ." In the process of our accepting the gift of salvation that is available because of the grace of God – grace is when we get something we don't deserve – we are "made alive in Christ," "raised up in Christ," and "seated with Him in the heavenly realms." So, right now as a follower of Jesus, we are physically seated on this Earth in the natural realm, but, spiritually, we are seated at the right hand of God in Christ. I keep asking Father God to give me more revelation as to what this really means.

Chapter 1 — **The Seat**

In our own human ways of thinking, this doesn't make sense, so it is hard to understand. We need to remember that we are three-part beings – body, soul and spirit. Even though the spiritual realm, which our spirit is meant to connect with, is not visible to us like the physical world, it is still very real. Think of it like the wind. We can't see the wind; but we can see the effects of the wind all around us when it is blowing (John 3:8). In our time, there is a growing interest in the reality of the spiritual realm. My desire is to grow in my understanding and experience in this realm. After all, my spirit is seated with Christ in the heavenly realms.

I would encourage each of you to also ask our loving, heavenly Father to give you more revelation on this. I really feel there is something so significant in our understanding of this that it will radically change how we view everything that happens around us.

Remember, where you are seated determines your perspective

How does being seated with Christ in the heavenly realms at the right hand of God change my perspective? My experience has been that, as I set my heart and mind on things above, as stated in Col. 1:1-2, life begins to look very different. Just like the person who observed the accident mentioned earlier from the 10th floor of a building; now, I am observing life from a higher perspective. When I realize that I'm seated at the right hand of God in Christ, I am able to look at the bigger picture of life and not be so focused on each little thing that happens to me throughout the day. When I realize that I am seated beside the Living God who created the whole universe; and, one day, will judge the living and the dead (1 Peter 4:5), I am able to let go of the judgments that I have against others. I am able to let go of a lot of things that brought a great deal of burden

Chapter 1 — The Seat

and stress to my life.

This brings incredible freedom to our lives. When we can get out of seats that we aren't called to sit in, and understand that our rightful place as followers of Jesus is to be seated with Christ in the heavenly realm, it changes our lives!

What are some of the seats we sit in and we need to get out of, to find freedom? In my own life, I know I have sat in the seat of judgment, the seat of bitterness, the seat of criticism, the seat of pride, the seat of worry, the seat of unbelief, the seat of what other people might think, the seat of being a victim, the seat of self pity, and the list could go on and on. If I sit in these seats, then my perspective on everything that happens and everyone I meet is determined from this seat.

Let's take a look at how things look if we sit in the seat of judgment. I have sat in this seat and encountered others who have as well. When in this seat, I have a lot of strong opinions; which, in most cases, are opinions I don't need to have. I have met people sitting in this seat and found these judgments to be very alienating. That is, unless we agree with their judgments. Then, we have a new best friend. You know the saying, "Birds of a feather flock together"? As followers of Jesus, we are called to choose life in each situation. Sitting in the seat of judgment is not life-giving to the one sitting in it, or anyone else influenced by them.

If I sit in the seat of being a victim, I view everything from the perspective that people are out to get me. In the seat of self-pity, I am never good enough. In the seat of criticism, there is something wrong that I complain about in every situation. In the seat of unbelief, everything looks impossible; and I am stuck with never moving forward into anything new.

When I get out of these seats and set my heart and mind on things above, life takes on a whole new perspective. The freedom that comes and the

Chapter 1 — **The Seat**

ability to enjoy every day, are simply amazing. There are incredible levels of peace and joy that God wants to give us as His children. These gifts can only be received when we get out of the seats we aren't called to sit in and take our rightful place in Christ. This requires that we learn new ways and develop new habits in our thinking.

Here is the problem that I see with many of us that are Christians. The Bible teaches us that we are seated with Christ at the right hand of God in the heavenly realms, as we see in the Ephesians and Colossians passages mentioned earlier; but, for one reason or another, we don't realize this. We come to Jesus, accept the gift of salvation and give our lives over to Him. Then, we continue on with life; but we haven't learned how to think and function as one who is in Christ seated in the heavenly realms. We need to learn new ways of thinking.

Let me explain it this way. Let us use the

example of driving a city bus as being seated with Christ in the heavenly realms. For those of us who drive city bus, it may be hard to think of a bus in this way; but, for sake of the example, try to work with me on this. If I came to work to do my job transporting people around the city and decided I didn't want to drive the bus, but that I could do my job by driving my car around the bus routes, what would happen? I could drive around on the routes all day and pick up a couple of people at a time, but I wouldn't be able to do my job to full potential because I wasn't using the right vehicle. I was not seated in the right place. You need to be in the right seat.

Now, if I drove the bus around the city for the day on all of my routes and was still thinking that I was driving my transport truck like I did in my previous job; how useful would I be? I would have lots of room on the bus but would only allow 1 person on at a time, because that's how many seats were in my truck. I would pull up to a stop

Chapter 1 — The Seat

with 10 people waiting and say, "I can only take 1 person." I would be not using the full potential of the vehicle I was driving because of not changing the way that I thought. When I started driving a bus, I needed to realize where I was seated and change my thinking accordingly.

I remember one time, when I stopped my bus at Fairview Mall, which is in Kitchener, a customer came to me and asked, "When will we be in Kitchener?" I replied that we were already there. I think that this is descriptive of how it is for us, sometimes, as Christians. I have heard someone say it this way: Most Christians are trying to get into a room that that they are already in. When we come to Jesus, we are a new creation; and, now, in Christ, we are seated in heavenly realms whether we realize it or not. We don't need to do anything more than what Jesus has done. If our thinking doesn't change to line up with our new position, we are like the example I gave of driving a bus but thinking that I am still driving a truck.

Where we are seated determines our perspective!

We need to learn what the Bible teaches us about our position in Christ and how that is lived out practically each day. I have found it helpful to regularly remind myself of my position in Christ. I am on a journey with this, and I invite you to join me in this journey.

Prayer:

Father God, thank You for Your great love for us that is demonstrated through Jesus Christ and for making us alive in Him. Thank You for seating us in the heavenly realms in Christ Jesus. I pray that You will give each of us, as your followers, a better understanding of what this means. Continue to show us how living life from this perspective changes how we live here on Earth.

Chapter 2
THE SIGN

"Does this bus go downtown?" "Does this bus go to the mall?" "Does this bus go to the school?" (I actually had a guy ask this exact question in a city with dozens of schools.) "Is this bus going to...?"

As bus drivers, we get asked a lot of questions throughout the day. I have often thought that, if you don't like answering questions, you should never be a bus driver! Most of the things we are asked can be summarized with this one question, "Where does this bus go?" I have learned that the process of answering this question is more efficient if I ask them where they want to go. Nonetheless, every one who gets on a bus wants to know where it is going.

This is the reason that all buses have a destination sign. On the front of the bus, above the windshield, there is a sign indicating what the destination of the bus is. There is also a smaller sign on the side of the bus with this info and an even smaller sign on the back of the bus with the only route number. These signs display and advertise to the world where the bus is going.

With each destination that is displayed on the sign, there is a specific route that I am expected to take to get to this destination. When people get on the bus, if they are familiar with the system, they know the route that I will take to get them to where they want to go. Many of our customers

Chapter 2 — The Sign

don't know the system very well, and that is why we get a lot of questions.

It is not uncommon that, when a bus leaves the terminal or a place of connecting with other buses, that there are gasps or expressions of, "Oh no!" when we make the first right or left turn. This isn't because we took the corner so fast that they almost fell out of their seat. No, it usually happens for two other reasons.

The first and most common reason is that the customer just realized they have gotten on the wrong bus. They thought this bus was going to Conestoga Mall, and now they realize it is going to the University. People get on the wrong bus everyday. Sometimes the realization that they are on the wrong bus doesn't come very quickly, and they may now be at the opposite end of the city from where they want to be. Many times, this has caused people to be late for work or appointments. This is why many have learned to ask questions when they get on the bus as to where to the bus is going. Many routes overlap parts of their route with other routes. At some bus stops, there can be 5 or 6 different routes that stop there. This makes the destination sign that much more crucial when getting on a bus.

The second reason is that the bus driver has made a wrong turn and is now off route. Like I mentioned earlier, there is a set route for me to drive for each of the destinations or routes that I have in a day. Making a wrong turn can happen very easily when you are driving different routes on the same day or week. Yesterday, I may have gone straight through the intersection at Fairway and King; and, today, I'm turning left there; and, next week, I could be turning right.

I hope this gives you a bit of an idea of how important knowing the route and the destination are to the driver and the customer. As drivers, we regularly need to remind ourselves of what route

Chapter 2 — The Sign

we are on so we make the appropriate turns.

When I have made a wrong turn, sometimes people yell out that I have gone off route. This has been done in nice, helpful ways and also in angry, condemning ways. This is particularly difficult when you are a new driver and you're learning the routes. I remember when I was in training, some students yelling from the back of the bus about how long it was taking for them to get home. My trainer that day was a driver who was known for freely expressing her opinions. She proceeded to clearly say to these students, "Relax! Have you ever been new at anything?"

There have been some occasions where I have made a wrong turn and the people on my bus have not said a thing. I remember one time when I realized several blocks down the road that I had missed my turn and was off route. When I apologized to the 5 or 6 people on my bus they responded with, "We were kind of wondering what you were doing," which got me wondering why they hadn't said something.

There are some customers who take it upon themselves to make sure the bus stays on route. I remember driving an early morning route, one time, that had a unique extension on one trip each day. A man got on and stood right behind me for 15 minutes. As we approached the corner where the bus would normally turn right, but on this trip was to go straight through, I put my signal on to turn right. Immediately he told me loudly that I was to go straight. I guess he had experienced too many times where a driver had missed the turn.

Another situation we sometimes have to deal with is a destination sign that is blank or doesn't work properly. The sign will, from time to time, not change when it is supposed to, so you, then, are driving a route that is contrary to what your sign says. When this happens, we need to

Chapter 2 – The Sign

let everyone who comes on the bus know where the bus is headed, so we can, hopefully, avoid confusion later on.

Lets look at what we can learn from the destination sign about everyday life. There are several things we can learn here:

Personal Destination Signs

Jesus talks about roads and destinations in:

Matthew 7:13-14

> [13] Enter through the narrow gate. For wide is the gate and broad is the road that leads to destruction, and many enter through it. [14] But small is the gate and narrow the road that leads to life, and only a few find it.

In this passage, Jesus talks about the wide road and the narrow road. There are only two options. We are either on the road to destruction or the road to life. From these verses, I would suggest to you that we all have a destination sign on us, indicating whether we are heading toward life or death. Now, this isn't always as visible as what a sign on a bus is; but it is still there. When we decide to follow Jesus and we surrender our life to Him, we are on the road that leads to life. Water baptism as a Christian is our public affirmation that we are followers of Jesus. Our destination sign is advertising to the world around us that we are on the narrow road headed towards life. If we have not decided to follow Jesus, we are on the road to destruction.

I have been a Christian most of my life as I accepted Jesus as my Lord and Saviour at age 11. I have talked to lots of people, over the years, that have walked away from God and the church. Many times, one of the reasons I have heard for this decision is because they have encountered Christians who are hypocritical. What is a hypocrite? Simply put, it is someone who says one thing and does another. In other words, it

Chapter 2 — The Sign

is someone who has not lived according to what they are advertising on their destination sign.

When the sign on me is advertising that my destination is life, I can't just live my life any way I want to anymore. There is a certain route that I must take. Just as when my destination sign on the bus says 7C Conestoga Mall and people have a certain expectation of the route I will drive to get there, so it is with my life when I declare to others that I'm a follower of Jesus. If my sign says 7C Conestoga Mall; but I decide I don't want to drive that route today and start to go on the route for the 1 Stanley Park, there will be problems. We must live our lives in ways that are congruent with what we are advertising on our sign!

Let's look at some more verses from that will help to explain this.

> Colossians 3:5-10
>
> [5] Put to death, therefore, whatever belongs to your earthly nature: sexual immorality,

> impurity, lust, evil desires and greed, which is idolatry. ⁶ Because of these, the wrath of God is coming. ⁷ You used to walk in these ways, in the life you once lived. ⁸ But now you must also rid yourselves of all such things as these: anger, rage, malice, slander, and filthy language from your lips. ⁹ Do not lie to each other, since you have taken off your old self with its practices ¹⁰ and have put on the new self, which is being renewed in knowledge in the image of its Creator.

In these verses, we see that, when we decide to follow Jesus, there are some things that we can no longer do. Things like sexual immorality, impurity, lust, evil desires, greed, anger, rage, malice, slander, filthy language, and lying all need to go. In the analogy that we are using of bus routes and destinations, I would say these are roads we no longer are to travel on. These "streets" are no longer on our route. If my sign is declaring that I'm a follower of Jesus and I go off route onto one of these streets, it is often obvious

Chapter 2 — The Sign

to everyone around me.

The Bible is very clear in teaching us that, when we come to Jesus, there is distinct change. Verses 9 and 10 of the Colossians 3 passage talk about taking off the old and putting on the new. We also see this in

> 2 Corinthians 5:17
>
> Therefore, if anyone is in Christ, that person is a new creation. The old has gone, the new is here!

This is a theme throughout Scripture. There is a letting go of the old and putting on of the new. I used to live a certain way; and now, as a follower of Jesus, I live differently. When we decide to follow Jesus, the process of transformation begins in our lives. I have a different destination so the streets I drive on have changed.

Now, none of us are perfect; and we all make mistakes. What we do when we make mistakes is crucial. When I make a wrong turn in my bus and a customer yells out, "Hey, Driver, you missed your turn!" my response determines how the conversation goes after this. I can say, "Mind your own business," or, "I didn't do anything wrong," which will not prove to be very helpful. If I, instead, respond with humility by saying, "You're right; I did miss my turn. Thanks so much for letting me know. We will get back on route shortly," this gentle and humble response always bears much better fruit.

So it is, when we make mistakes in life. If I go off route by getting angry, becoming greedy, being dishonest, or lusting after things that aren't mine, my attitude when confronted with these sins will determine the course of my life. It will also determine the influence, good or bad, that my life has on others. We each need to take responsibility for our actions and how they affect others. We don't live in a vacuum.

There have been times in my life where I have been "off route" and I have needed someone

Chapter 2 — The Sign

to confront me. Sin has a way of deceiving us into thinking that we are okay with the bad choices we are making. That is why it says in

Galatians 6:7

Do not be deceived: God cannot be mocked. A man reaps what he sows.

Someone who is willing to confront you at these times can literally save your life. Similarly, I have had times where I observed a brother or sister that is heading down the wrong street. Most of the time, people have been glad for this confrontation. Maybe not right at first, but, eventually, they are grateful. In both of these situations, an attitude of humility is the key to getting back on the right road.

I think that this is why some people don't want to let others know that they are Christians. If no one really knows what my destination sign says, I have a lot more freedom to take any route I choose. Having no accountability to anyone seems attractive to many. This is not the way Jesus taught us to live. Being a follower of Jesus is not meant to be something that is kept private or a secret. Jesus tells us in

Matthew 5:13-16:

[13] You are the salt of the Earth. But if the salt loses its saltiness, how can it be made salty again? It is no longer good for anything, except to be thrown out and trampled underfoot.

[14] You are the light of the world. A town built on a hill cannot be hidden. [15] Neither do people light a lamp and put it under a bowl. Instead they put it on its stand, and it gives light to everyone in the house. [16] In the same way, let your light shine before others, that they may see your good deeds and glorify your Father in heaven.

There are a few things I want to address as we use this analogy. First of all, I don't want you to read this and interpret this as an endorsement of religious legalism or a performance-based

Chapter 2 — The Sign

relationship with God. This can so easily happen when we talk about our responsibility to live correctly. This leads to one thinking that they do good things to earn right standing before God. We don't do what is right to earn God's love. Instead, we do what is right because we have received this incredible love from God. A true revelation of Father God's love for us changes us in ways that nothing else can. No longer is our life based on a list of rules and striving to keep them. Now, we have freedom to live in response to the greatest love in the world!

Secondly, we don't live our lives as followers of Jesus to please other people. We live to please Jesus Christ, the one who laid down His life for my sins and yours. Such love, the world has never known! I seek to make right choices in every situation because of this great love.

Do you know if you are on the wide road or the narrow road as you go through life? Are you headed for life or for destruction? If you can't answer these questions with certainty, I want to let you know that you can know, beyond a shadow of a doubt, what is your eternal destination.

Romans 10:9-10, 13

> [9] If you confess with your mouth, "Jesus is Lord," and believe in your heart that God raised Him from the dead, you will be saved. [10] For it is with your heart that you believe and are justified, and it is with your mouth that you confess and are saved... [13] for, "Everyone who calls on the name of the Lord will be saved."

If we call on the name of the Lord, believe and confess, as is stated in these verses, we are on the narrow road with a destination sign of life! It's that simple. This is the start of the greatest adventure. If you are not sure, then say this prayer.

Jesus, I believe that You died on the cross for my sin and that God raised You from the dead. Jesus, I need you in my life. I want to be on Your

Chapter 2 – The Sign

road of life. I confess that I am a sinner and I need Your forgiveness. Please forgive me of my sin and make me clean. I give You my life and accept You as my Saviour and my Lord. Please fill me with Your Holy Spirit so that I can be Your witness here on this Earth.

If you said this prayer, then you are now a child of God! You are now on the narrow road that leads to life! I would encourage you to tell someone of your decision. You can contact Angie and me through our website, www.arisenow.ca as we would love to support and encourage you.

More Specific Personal Destination Sign

Generally speaking, we are all headed towards life or death, as indicated on our destination signs. I would like us to consider that we can have more specific details on the signs that are on our lives. What I am talking about is often referred to as your destiny, calling or purpose. Do you know what your destiny, calling and purpose are? If we have a clear understanding of this in our lives, it is very helpful. This will also help determine how we live each day and what we invest our time in. It determines what streets we drive on, using the route analogy.

If you don't have a clear sense of what your destiny and purpose are, life can feel like a bus that is wandering around the city without a clear destination. A lot of time is spent driving and the kilometres add up; but, really, you don't get anywhere. I have had times in my life like this. There have been times when I didn't have a vision for the future or a sense of destiny. You know they say that if you aim at nothing you will hit it every time! Initially, this feels like a good and safe option; but, eventually, the futility of it sinks in.

On the contrary, I have had times in my life where I have had a real clear sense of purpose and

Chapter 2 — The Sign

destiny. This "reason for being," then determines many things throughout the course of each day. Having a sense of who I am in Christ and who God has called and created me to be, is life changing.

If you lack clarity in what your purpose and destiny are, I would encourage you to ask yourself these questions. What do I enjoy doing? What are the things I am most passionate about? What are my hopes and dreams for the future? Or, how about this question I was asked when working through the Boot Camp of Christian Experts, "What would your life look like in 3-5 years if you could write any script with no restrictions?" One of the reasons that I wrote this book you are reading is because I asked myself these questions and spent time seeking Father God for answers. Jesus said that, as we seek, we would find. I urge you to do the same. Ponder these questions in prayer, and I know that you will receive more than you could ever ask or imagine. That's the way our God is.

> Ephesians 3:20
>
> Now to him who is able to do immeasurably more than all we ask or imagine, according to his power that is at work within us.

Group Destination Signs

I would like to look briefly at how this whole destination sign analogy works with a group, not just individually. When I go to different congregations to preach, I like to check out their history and their mission statement. I want to know what this group of believers is advertising to the people who are checking them out. A group's vision and mission statements are like destination signs for all those interested in "taking a ride on their bus." It builds expectation as to what will happen if they connect with this group. These destination sign statements determine many of

Chapter 2 — The Sign

the decisions that the group makes. If we don't have a clear vision and mission, then the group will have a hard time making decisions.

Recently, I was preaching to a congregation that had this vision statement on their website, "Finding the way together." When I saw this, I felt that it was rather vague. Finding the way to what? I shared with this congregation that it felt like getting on a bus that said it was heading west. No more details, just west. Now, west is a good direction; but it is very general and not very helpful in letting someone know if the bus will get them where they want to go.

The other challenge is that we need to be consistent with what we advertise about ourselves. I have a friend who decided he wanted to start attending church, so he looked up churches in the Yellow Pages. He went to the first one on the list and saw on the sign outside the church building that "All are Welcome." That sounded good, so he went inside for the service; and nobody talked to him. Now, thankfully, this friend is quite determined and didn't let this stop him so he kept coming back. Finally, after several weeks, someone talked to him; and later he joined this local church. Most people would never have come back the second time.

It is very important to have a clear destination sign and know the route that we, as individuals and groups, will take to get there. Driving a bus, in a lot of ways, is quite simple because the route has been set out for me. The more often I drive a route, the more natural it becomes. It is the same way as a Christian. The longer I follow Jesus and learn to hear His voice in each situation, the more natural it becomes. He longs to be in close relationship with each of His followers and guide them through each day. When we learn to live fully in this relationship, we live a fulfilled life.

Chapter 2 — The Sign

> *Prayer:*
>
> Thank You, Jesus, that we can be on the narrow road that leads to life because of You! Thank You that you have not left us here to figure out how to travel on this road by ourselves, but You have sent us the Holy Spirit to be our constant companion. Show each of us clearly the route that we are to take and give us the ability to live lives of integrity. Amen!

Chapter 3
THE SYSTEM

There are many buses in the system at Grand River Transit. Every weekday, during the peak period of the day, there are approximately 183 buses on the road in service. (This number regularly changes as service is adjusted to meet demand.) After I started driving bus, I soon realized that I am just one bus in a bigger system. I don't need to drive anybody else's bus. I just need to do the best job that I can with the bus that has been assigned to me.

Each bus in the system also has a schedule to keep. Someone has put a lot of thought and time into designing schedules for each bus that is on the road. There is a plan to have routes meet at connecting points around the city so that customers can transfer from one bus to another.

For example, recently, I was driving the "24 Highland." I was scheduled to leave Highland Hill Mall at 8:10 am. There was another bus, the "22 Laurentian," that would arrive right around my departure, with a lady that would want to catch my bus. She would run from the route 22 to my bus, and we would head downtown on Highland Rd. At the corner of Highland Rd. and Belmont St., where I was due at 8:16 a.m., this same lady would get off my bus and hope to catch the "8 Westmount," that was due at the same time. Most days, these connections were all made; but, as you can imagine with variables such as traffic and weather, things didn't always work.

Chapter 3 — The System

This same kind of situation happens thousands of times a day throughout the whole system of Grand River Transit, as customers connect with other buses. The only way this works is if each bus in the system does their part. Each bus has a role to play in helping customers get to where they need to go.

Occasionally, a scheduled bus does not show up on time. This causes those waiting for the bus to get quite concerned. This can happen for a variety of reasons. When you are waiting for a bus that doesn't show up, it doesn't really matter why it isn't there. The only thing that matters is that you will most likely be late for wherever you are heading.

Some buses in the system are very busy and have lots of customers all day long. Other buses are on routes that are not very busy and may be mostly empty at times. Every bus picks up somebody. Every bus is needed to make the system work. There isn't a bus that never picks up customers. Is one bus more valuable to the system than another? I would say, "No," because, if each bus doesn't do the route assigned to it, someone will be affected.

What can we learn from the transit system that applies to our everyday life?

In the Bible, the analogy of a body is used to describe the followers of Jesus.

1 Corinthians 12:12-26

[12] Just as a body, though one, has many parts, but all its many parts form one body, so it is with Christ. [13] For we were all baptized by one Spirit so as to form one body—whether Jews or Gentiles, slave or free—and we were all given the one Spirit to drink. [14] Even so the body is not made up of one part but of many.

[15] Now if the foot should say, "Because I am not a hand, I do not belong to the body," it would not for that reason stop being part of the body.

Chapter 3 — The System

[16] And if the ear should say, "Because I am not an eye, I do not belong to the body," it would not for that reason stop being part of the body. [17] If the whole body were an eye, where would the sense of hearing be? If the whole body were an ear, where would the sense of smell be? [18] But in fact God has placed the parts in the body, every one of them, just as he wanted them to be. [19] If they were all one part, where would the body be? [20] As it is, there are many parts, but one body.

[21] The eye cannot say to the hand, "I don't need you!" And the head cannot say to the feet, "I don't need you!" [22] On the contrary, those parts of the body that seem to be weaker are indispensable, [23] and the parts that we think are less honourable we treat with special honour. And the parts that are un-presentable are treated with special modesty, [24] while our presentable parts need no special treatment. But God has put the body together, giving greater honour to the parts that lacked it, [25] so that there should be no division in the body, but that its parts should have equal concern for each other. [26] If one part suffers, every part

suffers with it; if one part is honoured, every part rejoices with it.

When we think of our physical bodies, every part is important. Every body part needs to do the job that they were created to do. Every part needs to be glad for their role and not wish they were some other part. A body functions in beautiful unity when every part does what they were created to do.

It is the same in the body of Christ. Every part is needed. We tend to celebrate the more visible parts – those with the more public roles – which makes the other parts feel less valuable. The heart of Jesus for His body is described really well in

Ephesians 4:11-16

[11] So Christ Himself gave the apostles, the prophets, the evangelists, the pastors and teachers, [12] to equip His people for works of service, so that the body of Christ may be built up [13] until we all reach unity in the faith and in

Chapter 3 — The System

the knowledge of the Son of God and become mature, attaining to the whole measure of the fullness of Christ.

[14] Then we will no longer be infants, tossed back and forth by the waves, and blown here and there by every wind of teaching and by the cunning and craftiness of people in their deceitful scheming. [15] Instead, speaking the truth in love, we will grow to become in every respect the mature body of Him who is the head, that is, Christ. [16] From Him the whole body, joined and held together by every supporting ligament, grows and builds itself up in love, as each part does its work.

I love the emphasis in these verses about the whole body growing and being built up. Verse 13 says, "…until we all reach unity." I also really like the phrase in verse 16, "every supporting ligament." Many years ago, I blew out my right knee and had ACL reconstruction done. My knee is great today, but only because every supporting ligament is in place. The ligament refers to a part that isn't visible but is so essential to the functioning of a body.

There is another passage that is helpful in understanding this.

Hebrews 10:24-25 (NKJV)

[24] And let us consider one another in order to stir up love and good works, [25] not forsaking the assembling of ourselves together, as is the manner of some, but exhorting one another, and so much the more as you see the Day approaching.

We have a beautiful description here of the body encouraging one another. I love the phrase, "Let us consider one another…" Encouragement needs to be done intentionally and carefully thought out; and the result is love and good works. Then we are told not to, "forsake the assembling of ourselves." Some translations of the Bible use the word, "gathering," or "meeting together," instead of "assembling." I really like the

Chapter 3 — The System

use of the word, "assembling," here because there is an important truth we can learn from it.

I have heard it explained this way. What is the difference between a gathering and an assembly? We can see the difference when we look at a bicycle. I have put a lot of bicycles together over the years. When the bike comes, it is in a box. All the parts are there; there is a gathering of the parts. This gathering of the parts is nice, but the bike will not serve any useful purpose at this point. The bike cannot accomplish that for which it was intended until the whole bike is assembled. Now, after the bike has been assembled, with all the parts put in their proper place, the bike is ready to be used.

In this season, the body of Jesus Christ, the church, is being assembled together with each part taking its place. We are moving past the times of just a gathering of the parts, into a time when each part will know its purpose and will function in beautiful unity with the other parts. It is a great joy when someone discovers what their purpose is and how they fit in the body.

> *Prayer:*
>
> Jesus, I ask that each one who is reading this book would know they have a part to play in the system. Give each one of us a revelation of what our purpose is. I pray that, as Your body is being assembled with each part taking it's place, the Church would rise up in power to be all that You ever intended. For those that are struggling with feelings of inadequacy, inferiority and uncertainty, I ask that You will replace these things with a vision of destiny, purpose and hope for the future! Amen!

Chapter 4
THE SECRET

Some days, while driving the bus, it feels like I am in a battle zone. There are times when this feels quite intense. The road might be filled with traffic, the bus crammed full of customers, and I'm running 5 minutes late. All the lights seem to be turning red as I approach them. Just ahead of me, there may be a lane closure due to construction, so traffic is now stop and go. A customer starts to yell at me that they are going to miss their connecting bus at the terminal and be late for work. I just had to brake hard because a person ran across the road in front of my bus without looking at all. I have a bell for the next stop meaning I have to stop there. The customer wanting off is a man in a wheelchair. Now, as the bus is full, everyone standing between him and the door needs to get off the bus and then get back on, once the wheelchair has gotten off. There is a car behind that is trying really hard to get past me. They are honking at me because my large vehicle is partially blocking their lane because of the narrow lanes on this road. Now, they see an opening; and they speed past me while honking the horn, yelling profanities out the window and waving their hand at me with only one finger sticking up. Bus drivers call this being told that we are number 1! Happens all the time.

All of what I just described can literally happen within minutes on any given day, while driving a city bus. Dealing with all of these things

Chapter 4 — The Secret

is one reason that I like the job. It is rarely boring, and every day is a new adventure.

In the midst of all this, there are some things that happen that really irritate me. Shortly after I started driving bus, I realized that something was happening to me. A car could do something that would cause my heart rate to race, like making a right turn right in front of me from the left lane at about 40 km/h. Another time, a car was so eager to pass me that they roared past my bus only to spin out at the upcoming sharp turn in the road. They were now facing me and in my way.

When these kind of situations happened, I would start to feel very agitated, angry and whole variety of other emotions. The car would only be in my sight, in most cases, for a very short time. They would disappear; and I would, most likely, never see this person again. Minutes later, or even hours afterward, I would still be thinking about what happened. Even though my heart rate had settled down, I could still feel all emotions as if it had just happened.

I began to realize that, if I was going to enjoy my job as a bus driver, I would need to handle things differently. It was in this process that I regularly started saying, to myself, three simple words.

LET IT GO!

These three words, I discovered, are the secret to, not only enjoying life as a bus driver, but also enjoying all of life! I would say this over and over to myself throughout the day, and what a difference this would make. I suppose I had known this for most of my life; but working in this job, took the understanding of this to a whole new level. It seemed so simple, but it changed everything. As I said these words I would be releasing anger, bitterness, judgments,

Chapter 4 — The Secret

and variety of other feelings that do not bear good fruit in my life.

When I would talk with other bus drivers that had several years of experience at this job, I learned that many of them had learned this same secret. Then there were other drivers who, for whatever reason, didn't release these things. These were usually the ones who didn't enjoy their job, wanted everyone else to know it, and support them in their bitterness. It is hard enough to let go of all the things in my day. Now I had to also be aware of the danger of picking up other people's offences.

Most of the things needing to be 'let go' come from relating with other people. Now, I don't have much of a relationship with the person in the car that cut me off, or the person that ran out in front of my bus; but, at a very basic level, I am relating to them. You may think it is easy to let go of things that happen between two people that have a very limited, and, in lots of cases, a short relationship or interaction. I would like to suggest to you that our ability to let things go with people we don't know very well will give us lots of practice for letting things go in closer relationships, like family and good friends. This helps us to develop good habits of releasing things and other people that have wronged us.

You can hear from others that letting things go is a key to life; but to really learn the lesson, you need to try it out for yourself. I discovered that when I'm able to let things go, I can have peace and joy flowing in my life that would otherwise not be there. Releasing these things very soon after they happened, I found was also very helpful. The longer I would hold on to the emotions, the harder it would be to let it go. The longer I hold on to something, the greater chance of what the Bible calls a 'bitter root,' will be established in my life.

Chapter 4 — The Secret

Hebrews 12:15

See to it that no one falls short of the grace of God and that no bitter root grows up to cause trouble and defile many.

I have seen the effect of bitter roots in my life and that of others. They always cause trouble; and, like the verse says, will defile many. Bitterness is like a poison in our bodies and in our relationships with others. The more we can do to keep bitterness from taking root in our life, the better off we will be.

There is an interesting verse in

Proverbs 18:19

A brother offended is harder to win than a strong city, And contentions are like the bars of a castle. (NKJV)

I have encountered exactly this. When we hold on so tightly to the wrong that someone has done to us, we become what this verse describes, an offended brother or sister. Often times, these offences start off quite small and seemingly insignificant. The longer they are held, the more likely that a bitter root will start to grow. What started as something small has now grown into a stumbling block that will destroy our relationships – and us.

This three-word phrase that I refer to as, "the secret," will work for each one of us in every area of life. There is such freedom in saying, "Let it go." I have even found that, anytime I have things stirring in me about an event or person, or if I am just feeling stressed out to the point where I am starting to have headaches, that simply saying to myself, "I release everything," changes things immediately. The headache leaves, and I am free! This doesn't change the circumstances I am in, but it changes the attitudes that I have.

Remember from the 1st chapter that, where

Chapter 4 — The Secret

you are seated determines your perspective. When we realize that we are seated in the heavenly realm in Christ Jesus, suddenly, it is a whole lot easier to let go of things here on this Earth, that seem so important to us.

The verses in Colossians are helpful in understanding this

Colossians 3:12-14

> [12] Therefore, as God's chosen people, holy and dearly loved, clothe yourselves with compassion, kindness, humility, gentleness, and patience. [13] Bear with each other and forgive one another if any of you has a grievance against someone. Forgive as the Lord forgave you. [14] And over all these virtues put on love, which binds them all together in perfect unity.

I love how these verses start off calling us, "God's chosen people, holy and dearly loved." This is a great description of how Father God feels about His children. In verse 13, the first words are, "Bear with one another."

This indicates that we can expect to have some challenges in our relationships with each other. When differences come up, or we hurt each other, we are called to forgive each other, just as the Lord forgave us. Wow, those are powerful words!

This also brings to mind what Jesus said in what we commonly refer to as the 'Lord's Prayer.' Jesus says in

Matthew 6:12

And forgive us our debts, as we also have forgiven our debtors.

When we pray this prayer, we are asking Father God to only extend to us the same level of forgiveness that we extend to others. Stop and think about that statement. Does it really mean that if I won't forgive others God can't forgive me?

Chapter 4 — The Secret

I would say, "Yes; that is true." Unforgiveness puts me in a prison, and I'm the only one with the key. Not even God has the key to this prison cell. (See Matthew 18.) He has set out the requirements for my freedom, and it all starts with my forgiveness that I give to those that have wronged me. Here the phrase, "Let it go," is the key that unlocks the door to our freedom.

I have had my share of conflict with other people over the years. With this, I have experienced times when things haven't always been able to be resolved to the level I would have liked. I always try to own up to my part and ask for forgiveness. It doesn't always happen quickly or easily, but I also want to live in complete forgiveness to others for anything that they have done to me.

One of my goals in life is to keep my heart totally free. I want to be able to go through life and be free to relate people without tensing up inside when I see them. I have had times when I meet up with people, and there is something in my heart that is not free. I continue to declare, in my heart, forgiveness towards that person. "Let it go; let it go; let it go," I have to say to myself. Then, when I see the person and there is no little twinge in my heart, I know that I am free. I remember a time when this happened; and, the first time I saw this person and I felt free, I didn't even think of it right away. Some time later, it dawned on me that I was free in my heart towards this person. Immediately, the words of a Chris Tomlin worship song came to mind; "My heart is free; no chains on me!!!!"

We can learn some more about this from

Colossians 3:15-17

[15] Let the peace of Christ rule in your hearts, since as members of one body you were called to peace. And be thankful. [16] Let the message of Christ dwell among you richly as you teach and admonish one another with all wisdom

Chapter 4 — The Secret

through psalms, hymns, and songs from the Spirit, singing to God with gratitude in your hearts. [17] And whatever you do, whether in word or deed, do it all in the name of the Lord Jesus, giving thanks to God the Father through him.

I love the phrase, "Let the peace of Christ rule in your hearts," in verse 15. If I want to have my heart completely free, as stated earlier, I need to let this peace "rule in my heart." I decide, many times a day, when I say, "Let it go," that the peace of Christ will rule in my heart. I have determined that I won't let anything steal my peace. When I refuse to let things go, I forfeit the peace that is mine as a follower of Jesus. This is the peace that is beyond comprehension, transcending all understanding (Philippians 4:7). Don't even try to understand it, because you can't. It is meant to be experienced, not understood.

Letting go and forgiving is not always an instant thing, and, many times, happens over a period of time. It is not an event, but a process; but it starts with a decision to let it go. After we make this decision, God, through the Holy Spirit, can continue to work in us to complete the process. The freedom that we experience when we totally let go and forgive is absolutely amazing!

The last part of verse 15 is, "and be thankful." In verse 16 and 17, the words, "gratitude" and "giving thanks" are used. Having a thankful heart is also a key to having the peace of Christ rule in our hearts. In fact, I have experienced that there is usually a direct link between the peace in my heart and the level of gratitude I'm expressing. If I grumble and complain, then peace is far from me.

We can develop this attitude of gratitude by intentionally giving thanks everyday, even when we don't feel like it. Think of everything you can to be thankful for, and then, when you can't think

Chapter 4 — The Secret

of any more, think harder. If we work at this and practise, it will become natural. The difference it makes in our lives and our impact on those around us is amazing.

I have worked in the customer service industry for many years. My observation is this; the happiest people I deal with are the most thankful. We can always find things to be thankful about, and it will bless those around us. I love being around thankful people!

If we can learn the power of this secret to enjoying life, we will never regret it. The fullness of life that is available to us as followers of Jesus begins in the forgiveness that Father God gives us. It continues, then, as we pass along that same forgiveness to all those that offend us. When life is lived this way, it is hard to describe the freedom that we experience. The invitation is there for all to enter this most fulfilling journey!

Prayer:

Father God, I thank You for offering me forgiveness for my sins. Many times, it has been hard for me to extend that same forgiveness to those who have hurt me. I choose, this day, to declare to my soul, "Let it go!" I release all the hurts and extend forgiveness to all those who have offended me. I want to walk in complete freedom and have the peace of Christ rule in my heart. Thank You, Jesus! Amen.

CONCLUSION

I hope that, as you have read this book, you have been having thoughts about lessons you can learn about life from your daily job or things you experience every day. There is often great encouragement and learning as we ponder these things. There is much more that could be said about life as a bus driver and what we can learn from it. I hope this has not only encouraged you in your journey, but that you will remember the things we have talked about regarding The Seat, The Sign, The System, and The Secret in those moments in the future when these lessons will help you in some way.

If you enjoyed this book please tell others about it. As well, check out my other book in this series entitled, "Lessons Learned on the Seat of My Bike."

I wish all of you much blessing as you go through life. Keep developing your relationship with Jesus. Following Jesus is the most exciting adventure we can ever have.

One more thing – always be nice to bus drivers!

More About
PAUL & ANGIE WAGLER

Paul Wagler is an inspired preacher with a gift of encouragement, an approachable way to connect with people, and an awesome ability to quote scripture. An avid cyclist in both mountain bike and road disciplines, Paul also manages a mountain bike team. He has worked in the transportation industry, as a bus operator and truck driver.

Paul and his wife Angie are the founders of Arise Now — a ministry to encourage and equip.

They have been church planters and pastors, and have been involved in church in various forms including traditional, cell, house churches and leadership healing groups. They understand wilderness pruning and fine-tuning and have an understanding of walking through the painful process that pre-empts inheritance.

Happily married for almost 30 years, they make their home in Kitchener, Ontario, Canada. They have three grown children and one much loved dog.

Paul and Angie would love to hear how this book has impacted you. You can contact them through their website: **www.arisenow.ca** or the Arise Now facebook page.

ONE LAST THING...

If you enjoyed this book and found it helpful we would love if you would post a short review on Amazon. Thanks!

OTHER BOOKS AVAILABLE
—BY PAUL WAGLER

Lessons Learned on the Seat of my Bike —Volume 2

You will want to read this gem to find out some of this mountain bikers secrets to help you successfully navigate your life's course!
Available in both kindle and paperback versions on Amazon.

What others are saying...

Paul Wagler has done it again! A dynamic follow-up to his first book, "Lessons Learned on the Seat of My Bus: Secrets to Enjoying Life No Matter What Happens!", you'll enjoy how Paul delivers life changing lessons for avid cyclists, non-riders, mountain bikers, fair-weather riders, and everyone else in between. Ride along with Paul as he authentically shares the joys, the pains, the victories, and the mistakes he has experienced—on and off these non-motorized two wheels—so that you can gain gold nuggets about living a life that matters, pressing on, and finishing well. You'll even discover why you don't want a DNF or a DNS beside your name. Enlightening, practical and thought-provoking, well worth the read.
    —Jackie Morey, COO of Customer Strategy Academy;
    www.Your21stCenturyBusinessCard.com, www.CustomerStrategyAcademy.com, www.Your90DayLaunchpad.com

Paul's life can serve as an example for all of us. His use of stories from his biking experiences, to illustrate simple yet deep truths, is outstanding. He takes the complex and makes it simple. His book is a must read.
    —David Powers, Author and Coach; www.fear-to-faith.com

I enjoyed reading Paul's book. He has biking illustrations that fit pretty much all of life! And they are great illustrations! I feel myself limping as he runs with his bike shoes to the finish line! It's amazing!!
    —Jim Loepp Thiessen, Pastor

—BY ANGIE WAGLER

Go on a journey with Jesus in

All my ROOMS

He is knocking on your door and wanting you to invite him in to all your rooms. Find out what He will say and impart to you that will bring transformation to your heart and life! Available in kindle and paperback on Amazon.

What others are saying...

Angie Wagler's book *All My Rooms* is a delightfully practical look at life. By comparing a room of your house to a part of your life, she enables you to invite Jesus in and assist you in every way.

The Living Room correlates to our thought processes. The Family Room speaks of relationships, and how to forgive. From The Bedroom: "To sleep well, we need to put fear in its place!" Her personal story of doing this is greatly encouraging.

At the end of each chapter, Angie invites us to take some time to write down our own reaction to her teaching. This engaging book is one you will want to use over and over. Even as we sometimes move from place to place physically and need to "redecorate," at times, we also have to move in our thinking. All My Rooms gives a refreshing way for a spiritual spring cleaning and refocusing of our lives.

—Jane Huff, Author, An Intimate Look at the Armor of God: Finding Safety in a Broken World

Watch also for Volume 2 in the Transformation Series

The **WILDERNESS TRAINING** Manual

a resource to bring freedom from the slavery mindset and to access the promises of God!

Made in the USA
Charleston, SC
19 March 2016